COPING™

T0034710

COPING WITH
THE THREAT OF
DEPORTATION

Jeanne Nagle

Rosen
YA™

New York

Published in 2019 by The Rosen Publishing Group, Inc.
29 East 21st Street, New York, NY 10010

First Edition

Library of Congress Cataloging-in-Publication Data

Names: Nagle, Jeanne, author.
Title: Coping with the threat of deportation / Jeanne Nagle.
Description: New York : Rosen Publishing, 2019. | Series: Coping | Includes bibliographical references and index. | Audience: Grades 7–12.
Identifiers: ISBN 9781508179115 (library bound) | ISBN 9781508179108 (pbk.)
Subjects: LCSH: Illegal aliens—Government policy—United States—Juvenile literature. | Deportation—United States—Juvenile literature. | United States—Emigration and immigration—Government policy—Juvenile literature.
Classification: LCC JV6483.N35 2019 | DDC 325.73—dc23

Manufactured in the United States of America

CONTENTS

INTRODUCTION

Immigration policy, which concerns people living and working in a country other than the one in which they were born, has been debated the world over for centuries. Yet the topic has become quite a hot-button issue of late, particularly within the United States. The political and economic climate in the United States has given rise to calls for overhauling the nation's immigration laws and/or better enforcing those already in place. The result would be stricter limits regarding the number and nationality of immigrants allowed into the country.

Of particular concern is what should be done about people from other countries who attempt to enter, or are already in, the United States illegally. These are people who, for a variety of reasons, have not gone through proper channels and obtained the paperwork necessary to be considered official temporary residents or permanent citizens. In the United States, such undocumented immigrants have been targeted for removal under a system known as deportation.

Being removed from the United States and sent back to one's country of origin obviously is a problem for the person being deported. Whether they are traveling legally or illegally, immigrants tear up roots and basically give up everything they know when they move to a new country. When undocumented immigrants are forced to leave their adopted homeland

Undocumented immigrants walk in the desert after entering the United States from Mexico. Those caught entering the United States illegally may be subject to deportation.

as well, it can feel as if they are citizens of nowhere. They are unwelcome in their country of choice and, because often they are seen as foreigners, failures, or even "traitors" by their native kinsmen, it is difficult for them to start again in their birthland. In some cases, deportees have been living in the United States for so long that they no longer have any ties to, or even working knowledge of, life in their native land. This is especially true of children born in the United States to nondocumented immigrant parents.

But deportation affects more than just the deportee, in a variety of ways. It can separate families, including children from their parents. People's ability to earn a living or get an education can be jeopardized when a wage earner or head of household is deported. In fact, the mere possibility of being deported can cause trouble, stemming from having to live a life of fear and secrecy.

Deportation is a harsh reality for anyone living in a country that is not their own. Yet those affected are not powerless against this threat. Learning to cope with a bad situation is the best defense a person has in times of trouble. Potential deportees, as well as their family and friends, have at their disposal a number of coping methods that can help when facing removal. Tools in the coping arsenal include forming practical plans of action, seeking legal recourse, and taking steps toward emotional healing.

The threat of being removed from a country that has become a new homeland is certainly not a matter to be taken lightly. Yet with awareness of the issues at play, an honest assessment of the situation, and the willingness to meet any problems that arise head-on, the threat can be contained, or at least managed, in the lives of anyone eligible for deportation.

What, Who, and Why

In order to cope with a problem successfully, it is important to understand as much as possible about the situation, from start to finish. A technique used in journalism may help in this regard. Reporters often consider five important questions when trying to get to the bottom of a story: who, what, when, where, and why. Regarding the issue of deportation, the answer to the question "when" is most definitely "right now." The "where" could be any number of European and North American countries, but for the purposes of this book, the United States will be front and center.

That leaves what, who, and why. "What" is obviously deportation itself, including the laws and policies in place to combat illegal entry into the country. "Who" takes a look at the people affected by deportation, as well as the organizations and individuals involved in making and enforcing deportation policy. Finally, the "why" revolves around the reasons why immigrants might choose to enter the country illegally, as well as why deportation proceedings may be initiated.

The "What" of Deportation

In the simplest terms, deportation is legal and forcible removal from a country. Anyone who is considered a threat to the safety of the United States and its citizens may be deported. Any noncitizen is subject to deportation if he or she breaks the law or otherwise violates a country's immigration policy. It is not just undocumented aliens who can be deported from the United States. Even those who go through the process and receive legal documentation can be removed. Aliens who gain citizenship are referred to as naturalized citizens. They may be denaturalized if they are found to have committed a crime prior to being naturalized or knowingly gave false information to officials in their attempt to become naturalized citizens. Denaturalization is the same as being stripped of citizenship. A denaturalized citizen can be deported.

For the most part, natural-born citizens are exempt from removal. They can, however, lose their citizenship by actively renouncing their citizenship or otherwise showing that they are loyal to another country. Those who lose or let go of their US

An ICE agent watches as an undocumented immigrant boards a plane as part of deportation proceedings. There are many reasons why someone may be deported.

citizenship in this fashion are said to be expatriates, who are deportable.

Once a person is deported, it is extremely difficult for him or her to return to the United States legally. There is no way to return under a former visa. Basically, people start the immigration process over again from scratch—or for the first time, if they had been in the country as an undocumented alien. Depending on the circumstances of the deportation, a deportee typically must wait between five and twenty years before even attempting to reenter the United States. He or she also is required to have a request for reentry approved by the US attorney general's office. Those who were convicted of an aggravated felony or are caught trying to reenter illegally after being deported may be banned permanently.

The Immigrants in Question

The most obvious group of people involved in deportation policy and process has to be the undocumented immigrants themselves. Also included are their families, especially spouses and children. The Pew Research Center in Washington, DC, has put the estimated number of undocumented immigrants in the United States at around eleven million.

Overwhelmingly, the majority of immigrants attempting to enter and actually living in the United States come from Mexico, which makes sense because Mexico and the United States share a land border. Even though the border is well guarded, entering the United States on foot by land is still, technically, easier than trying to enter unnoticed traveling by sea or air.

Being forcibly removed from the United States can be especially hard on parents, who risk being separated from their American-born children if they are deported.

Immigrants come, both legally and illegally, to the United States and other countries for economic, political, and personal reasons. Coming to a new land for employment opportunities or attending school to earn an academic degree that leads to career success are the main economic factors regarding immigration. On the political front, immigrants may leave the

Points of Origin

Over the past decade or so, the undocumented immigration tide has changed, if ever so slightly. Research has shown that although Mexico still has the largest undocumented population in the United States, the overall number of Mexicans coming to the country through improper channels is on the decline. Meanwhile, several Central American and Asian countries have numbers in the same category that are on the rise. Guatemala, El Salvador, and Honduras take the top spots from Central America, and Asian countries are represented mainly by China, India, and Korea. This shift has not affected the total number of undocumented immigrants in the United States, which has stood at approximately eleven million for years.

country in which they were born because of war or governments restricting freedoms and threatening or harming their citizens. When this happens, people typically seek asylum, which is asking to stay in the United States for protection and security. Wanting to reunite with family members and other loved ones in another country counts as a personal reason someone may choose to migrate.

This sign warns motorists to watch out for people crossing a US highway near the Mexican border. Entering the country illegally is dangerous, but millions are willing to risk it.

In short, immigration is largely a story of people trying to attain better, safer lives for themselves and their families. It can be argued that, in their attempt to achieve their goals, some people take chances and shortcuts and disregard immigration laws, thereby entering a country illegally.

Roadblocks to Legality

United States immigration policy generally favors three paths leading to legal entry. Employer-based immigration is when a company or business sponsors an alien to enter the country for work. Foreign applicants have to prove they are qualified for the jobs being offered, which are usually in specialized fields that require a high degree of education. Visas are also issued in the name of family reunification. Documented immigrants sponsor, and at least temporarily support, relatives so that immediate family—typically parents, children, and grandparents—can be reunited and live together in the United States. Finally, special consideration is given to immigrants who have refugee status under humanitarian visas. These are people seeking asylum from political, religious, or some other type of persecution in their home country.

As shown, these three types of legal immigration come with a number of conditions, both surrounding the alien hopeful and the people and organizations who

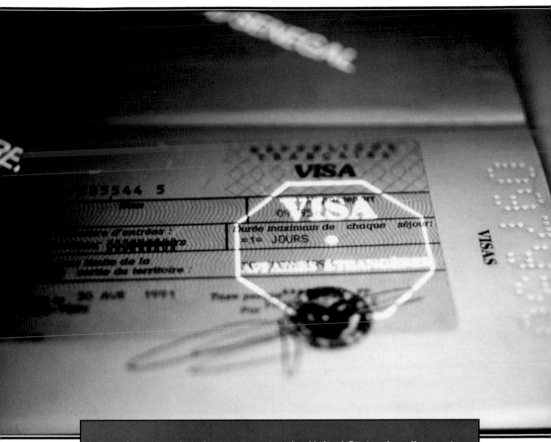

Immigrants who choose to enter the United States legally must obtain a visa, which spells out their legal status and how long they may stay in the country.

sponsor the person. Only a relatively small number of people can meet all these requirements. Further complicating matters is the fact that the number of each type of visa is extremely limited in the United States, as is the total number of immigrants allowed into the country during any given year. The tremendous limits placed on being able to immigrate legally to the United

States as well as years-long wait times to obtain such visas by those who qualify are two reasons so many people opt to risk coming to the United States illegally.

Policy Sources

In the United States, immigration policy is normally dictated by the federal government—in particular, the legislative branch or US Congress. As with other bills and legislation, immigration laws are proposed and voted on by members of the Senate and House of Representatives. Once approved, bills are sent to the sitting president, who can either sign them into law or veto them. Throughout the nation's history, the states have passed some laws that have affected immigration within their own borders, but this is not the norm. The situation is much the same in Canada, where Parliament is charged with creating immigration policy and reform, but provinces are bound to have their say as well under the Canadian constitution.

US presidents can also influence immigration policy through executive orders. Such was the case in 2012 when President Barack Obama issued several executive orders regarding immigration, including the Deferred Action for Childhood Arrivals (DACA). Patterned after portions of the DREAM Act, a proposal that had been kicking around Congress in some form since 2001, DACA allowed undocumented immigrants

President Barack Obama meets with a group of "DREAMers" in 2015. The Deferred Action for Childhood Arrivals program was a presidential mandate issued by Obama in 2012.

who had come to the United States as children to apply for two-year deferments on deportation, provided they met certain requirements. In 2014, the Obama administration attempted to expand DACA and give deportation deferment to undocumented parents whose children were either legal US citizens or permanent residents under what became known as DAPA (Deferred

17

Action for Parents of Americans and Lawful Permanent Residents). Claiming both orders were unconstitutional, the Donald Trump administration rescinded first DAPA, then DACA, in 2017.

Agencies In Charge

Policing the flow of immigrants into the United States used to be the job of the Immigration and Naturalization Service, shorthanded to the INS, which came under the control of the US Department of Justice. After the terrorist attacks of September 11, 2001, in the United States, things changed. Operating under the Department of Homeland Security, established in 2002, three separate government agencies took over the various duties of the INS.

United States Citizenship and Immigration Services (USCIS) handles many administrative tasks involved with immigration and naturalization, which is the process of becoming a citizen of a new country. This involves reviewing and approving or rejecting a number of forms, including applications for citizenship and visas, as well as requests for asylum.

Customs and Border Protection oversees activity along the nation's borders. On the customs side, the agency inspects all items (shipments, packages, etc.) being brought into the country. It is also charged with checking immigration status. At all points of entry into the United States, border agents determine if aliens trying to enter the country are doing so legally. They are in charge of examining the paperwork of non-US citizens to determine if everything is in order and official. Border patrols stand watch over areas other than legitimate points of entry, making sure that no one sneaks into the country without going through proper channels. Border agents at any location are authorized to place suspected undocumented immigrants into custody for further questioning or to start deportation proceedings.

When it comes to deportation, the final agency of the three is the one that seems to get the most attention. Immigration and Customs Enforcement (ICE) does exactly as its name says: enforces immigration and customs laws and policy. The agency polices interior immigration crimes, meaning within the country's borders. In addition to illegal immigration, ICE also enforces laws against terrorism and drug and human trafficking. According to the agency's website, finding, detaining, and ultimately removing nondocumented aliens from the United States is ICE's "largest single area of responsibility."

Reasons for Deportation

As much as undocumented immigrants have their reasons for coming to the United States illegally, the

An ICE logo hangs outside a Texas detention center. Immigration and Customs Enforcement agents are on the front lines when it comes to deportation.

federal government has a list of reasons for deporting them. Of course, simply being in the country illegally or helping other people do the same are also grounds for detainment and deportation. Also high on the list is being undocumented and committing a crime or having a criminal record. Being in violation of one's legal alien status is another offense that could result in deportation proceedings, as is knowingly giving false information in an attempt to get a visa. The US government also can deport—or reject from entering right off the bat—anyone who receives certain types of public assistance, known as a public charge.

Secure Communities

Locating and deporting undocumented immigrants is a federal matter, meaning state and local police are not considered immigration enforcement officers. However, the federal officers of ICE depend on the cooperation of state and local law enforcement when it comes to sharing information about undocumented immigrants in their custody. In 2008, the US federal government established Secure Communities, a program that cemented partnerships among law enforcement at all levels

(continued on the next page)

(continued from the previous page)

with regard to identifying and deporting criminals among the undocumented alien population.

The program gave federal authorities electronic access to the fingerprints of those arrested at the local and state level. Federal immigration officers searched databases to identify criminals who were in the country illegally. Once identified, these individuals were turned over to immigration enforcement, which started deportation proceedings against them.

Participation in Secure Communities started off with a handful of local law enforcement agencies during the presidency of George W. Bush and grew under the administration of President Barack Obama. By 2013, the program was in effect in local jurisdictions across the nation, only to be discontinued in 2014 under immigration reform measures. President Donald Trump reintroduced the program in 2017, attempting to expand its reach beyond 2013 levels.

According to its pages on the Department of Homeland Security website, Immigration and Customs Enforcement ranks deportation-worthy offenses. After criminals, ICE lists those who have recently crossed US borders illegally, repeatedly violated immigration laws, and failed to show up for immigration hearings as "high priority" cases for their agency.

The Criminal Element

Homeland Security states that, first and foremost, the United States advocates the removal of "individuals who pose a threat to national security." That includes terrorists and violent felons. Among the felonies that warrant deportation are murder, firearms violations, and drug and human trafficking. The Pew Charitable Trusts and several immigration rights groups note that since 1988, under immigration law, the US Congress has added less serious crimes, such as theft, to the list of "aggravated felonies" that can get an undocumented immigrant deported. Further muddying the waters is the fact that individuals can be deported for crimes as they are newly added to the list. This is true even if the person has already served time or paid some other penalty for the crime in question.

Overstaying One's Welcome

Also on ICE's deportation radar are documented aliens who have violated the terms of their immigration status. Visas are issued on a permanent and temporary basis. Temporary nonimmigrant visas allow foreigners to work or study in the United

States, or visit as a tourist. Immigrant visas are issued to those who wish to become permanent residents. Conditional permanent resident visas are issued to immigrants who marry a citizen or are entrepreneurs investing (heavily) in US businesses. Conditions are placed on these documents to make sure that either the marriage or the business investment is legitimate and not some kind of scam to stay in the United States. On a related note, if immigration officials determine that a person married a US citizen in order to stay in the country, he or she has committed fraud and is subject to deportation.

Conditional permanent resident visas are good for only two years before they expire, and the holder must apply to have the conditions removed. One of the biggest ways people violate the terms of their status is to stay longer than permitted on a conditional visa or neglect to renew their temporary visa.

Falsified Documents

When people change or otherwise lie about information on legal, official paperwork, a felony called falsifying documents has occurred. Examples include changing the amount written on a check and putting one's picture on someone else's driver's license or other identification card. Another example is purposefully filling out an application using false

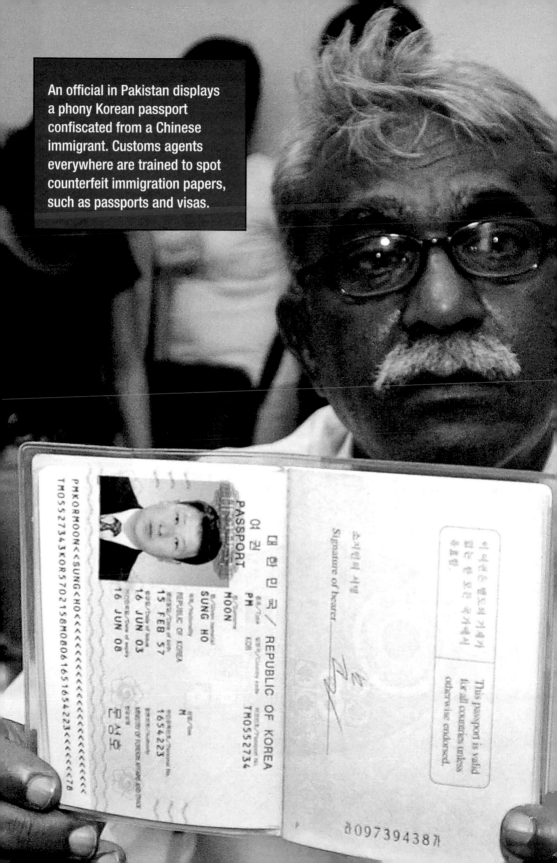

An official in Pakistan displays a phony Korean passport confiscated from a Chinese immigrant. Customs agents everywhere are trained to spot counterfeit immigration papers, such as passports and visas.

information in an effort to better one's chances at getting into the country legally. People entering the United States illegally may purchase or otherwise obtain fake visas to show to immigration officials as proof that they are in the country legally. They may give an employer a counterfeit Social Security card as a means to get or keep a job. Even those who attempt to enter the country legally may be guilty of falsifying documents if they knowingly lie on their visa application. As a criminal offense, falsifying documents in general is punishable by paying fines and/or serving jail time. Falsifying immigration documents usually also results in deportation.

Dependent on the Government

Immigrants seeking to legally enter the United States may be denied admission if officials decide they are likely to become a public charge, which is someone who depends on government money to survive. Documented permanent residents are banned from taking part in government assistance programs for five years after they have received their visa. This rule was established as a way to make sure immigrants could support themselves and contribute to the national economy, rather than be a drain on it. Traditionally, certain programs have been exempted, particularly those that benefit children such as school lunch programs. Although it isn't a regular occurrence, failure to abide by the five-year condition on permanent residence can result in deportation. In 2017, President Donald Trump drafted an executive order and issued a presidential memorandum that proposed widening the scope of who could be deemed a public charge. He also instructed the Department of Homeland Security to crack down on enforcement of the public charge rule.

CHAPTER TWO

The Deportation Process

In general, deportation proceedings are as unique as the individuals facing deportation. Depending on the circumstances, deportation can happen rather quickly, or it may take time as undocumented immigrants and their lawyers use every means at their disposal to prove they should stay in the country. Because of backlogged cases in immigration court, deportation proceedings may be delayed. During that time, and depending on the nature of the case, undocumented aliens may be allowed to return to their homes, or they may be detained in detention facilities or even jail.

Yet for all the differences, there is a certain similarity to cases as well. There is an involved procedure in place to handle the removal of undocumented immigrants from the United States. Depending on the circumstances of each individual's situation, either some or all of the steps for deportation to occur should be followed.

Canadian immigration agents prepare to take a Turkish family into custody as they attempt to enter Canada illegally. The United States is not the only country facing deportation issues.

Identify and Locate

Before the deportation process can begin, ICE agents identify who and where the undocumented immigrants are, separating them from those who are in in the country legitimately. Some immigrants attempting to enter the country illegally are revealed when they are

29

caught by Border Patrol agents at the moment they try to cross a border. Those who make it into the country are discovered in other ways.

Committing crimes or having a criminal record is a direct path to deportation. Undocumented aliens who commit an aggravated felony will, of course, get the attention of police and ICE pretty quickly. Lesser crimes, such as being pulled over for a traffic stop, might bring phony or nonexistent documentation to the attention of immigration officials.

Even something as simple as a phone call can lead to the start of deportation proceedings.

Since the events of September 11, 2001, citizens of the United States have been trained to report activity they believe may have ties to terrorism. Anyone who equates undocumented foreigners with terrorists might tip off the authorities that a neighbor or coworker is in the country illegally. If they are angry or somehow fear for their personal safety, even friends or family members might contact ICE about an undocumented immigrant. Homeland Security has established a twenty-four-hour tip line for individuals who want to report activity that may be linked to terrorism, drug smuggling, and a host of other felonies. People use that line and a related online "tip form" to report possible immigration violations as well.

Stings and Stingrays

In the United States, concerns over terrorism and crime have, from time to time, meant an uptick in immigration enforcement, resulting in more raids (also known as "targeted enforcement actions") on

ICE agents prepare to raid a house in California, looking for undocumented immigrants. Stepped-up immigration enforcement seems to be the wave of the future in the United States.

31

homes, neighborhoods, and workplaces in an attempt to remove criminals and threats from the country. Such has been the case under the Trump administration, which expanded the use of targeted enforcement actions, as well as the definition of who should be targeted in such raids.

Homeland Security and ICE officials have pointed out that the administration's directives have given them more freedom to do their job, which is the removal of dangerous criminals and threats to the nation's security. Opponents of the raids raise concerns that non-targeted individuals—people who have committed minor offenses (versus felonies) or who have no criminal record at all—are being swept up as well, putting them at risk of being deported along with their dangerous counterparts.

Immigrant advocacy groups also have sounded the alarm regarding the government's purported use of technology to identify and track undocumented immigrants. Chief among their concerns were reports that ICE was using what is known as stingray mobile call-intercepting devices to lead them to undocumented aliens. The devices allow cell phone usage to be traced and hacked, making apprehension of users much easier. The technology is approved for use by Homeland Security to catch criminals but only under a legally obtained warrant.

Immigration officials are increasingly turning to cell phones and other technology to locate—and deport—those who are in the country illegally.

The concern over stingray use to arrest and deport undocumented immigrants stemmed from a case where an undocumented man, who had returned to the United States after having been convicted of a felony and deported for that offense, was arrested and deported. A warrant had been issued in this case. However, advocates worried that this legal use of stingrays might open the door to wider use of the devices to focus on deportation issues rather than criminal ones. Also, they voiced the opinion that, as with the expanded target enforcement actions, non-targeted individuals might get rounded up in the process, despite there being no warrant for their cell phone information.

Arrest and Detainment

No matter how immigration offenses come to light, the end result is largely the same—arrest by immigration agents. Because they are locations where immigrants are likely to be found, homes and places of business are frequent sites for arrests. But undocumented aliens can be taken into custody just about anywhere—even in locations that used to be considered "sensitive," or relatively safe. These include schools, daycare facilities, places of worship, and hospitals and other medical facilities.

According to the Customs and Border Patrol website, agents should avoid enforcement action in such places, but exceptions are made if they have received approval from someone in a supervisory position at the location or if there are extenuating circumstances that could put the public or national security at risk. ICE and CBP agents are also officially discouraged from taking action at civil ceremonies, such as weddings and funerals, or during public demonstrations, meaning rallies or protests.

Arrest Developments

According to a report released by the Immigration and Customs Enforcement agency, ICE arrested more than 41,000 people for deportation-worthy offenses during the first six months of 2017. That number represented not only an increase in overall arrests in such matters but also a rise in the number of undocumented immigrants who had never been convicted of a crime. Ironically, the higher number of arrests did not correlate to more deportations. In fact, removals were actually down by about 12 percent from a similar timeframe the year before.

(continued on the next page)

(continued from the previous page)

Apparently, a large part of the problem was that immigration courts were overwhelmed by the number of cases before them and, to put it bluntly, could not process deportation orders fast enough.

Local and state police cannot arrest a person on immigration violations because they are not legal immigration officers. They can, however, arrest someone for other criminal complaints and then notify ICE that the person is in their custody. Often ICE will request that a suspected undocumented immigrant be kept in custody long enough to conduct their own investigation and interview the individual.

Being kept in custody is a state known as detainment. The length of detainment is determined largely by the offenses committed by an undocumented immigrant, as well as how much of a flight or safety risk the person is. Some detainees can be released after they have posted what is known as a delivery bond. This is an amount of money, typically a minimum of $1,500, given to the court in exchange for the person's freedom until his or her case is reviewed by an immigration judge. Paying a delivery bond also acts as a promise that the person will show up for any subsequent court

Local police have been tapped to help ICE agents remove undocumented immigrants from the United States. However, there is resistance by police in some cities to this tactic.

dates. Detainees may not be offered bond if they are considered a flight risk or if they pose an imminent danger to the safety of the general public.

Getting Detention

Undocumented immigrants who have been detained, but who either are not granted bond or cannot afford to pay it, are generally kept in detention centers while they wait for their deportation cases to be heard. The system of more than 200 US detention facilities includes jail-like compounds and actual jails themselves. Some of the non-jail facilities are run by ICE, which oversees

Detention facilities typically are as stark and crowded as a jailhouse, and often just as heavily guarded.

the entire immigration detention system. But it is estimated that approximately 65 percent of detainees ride out their detention in places built and run by companies as private prisons. Some of these privately owned facilities are located within prisons run by the same company.

Just as is the case with jails and federal penitentiaries, most detention centers house either men or women; a handful of "family detention facilities" hold women and their minor children, most of whom seek asylum. Detainees live under guard behind fences, and they are allowed few if any personal items.

The detainment period for those originally arrested by law enforcement agencies other than ICE or CBP cannot exceed forty-eight hours. People in immigration detention centers are detained until their deportation proceedings have concluded, which could take weeks, months, or even years.

Master Calendar Hearings

Every person arrested by ICE must be given a Notice to Appear. This document details why the individual has been arrested, what immigration laws have been violated that may result in deportation, and where/when the person is expected to show up in court for different hearings.

Deportation proceedings are overseen by an immigration judge, who listens to the cases presented by both sides and makes a decision without benefit of a jury.

After the receipt of a Notice to Appear, the first step in the removal process is a master calendar hearing. This is mainly an appearance before an immigration judge to review information about the situation, including a check of the immigrant's identity and a brief description of the charges against the person. The court will make sure that the person accused of being an undocumented alien understands why he or she is present and ascertain if help is needed with regard to hiring a lawyer—if one is not already present. Also, both parties are given a schedule of when written documents supporting their claims need to be submitted. More than one master calendar hearing may occur, depending on whether either side, the Department of Homeland Security and the person accused of being undocumented, can successfully argue that more time is needed to gather evidence and make a case.

At the conclusion of a master calendar hearing, the court will determine a date for everyone's next appearance before a judge. This can either be an additional master calendar hearing or what is known as a merits hearing. The latter is called a merits hearing because the immigration judge decides on the merits of the case against the defendant. In other words, whether he or she should be deported.

Sweet Relief

During a master calendar hearing, a defendant may make any number of requests that are referred to as discretionary relief. These are ways wherein someone can try to avoid getting deported or otherwise change the nature of the case against him or her. Discretionary relief includes asylum, withholding of removal, cancellation of removal, and voluntary departure.

Asylum

In order to be granted asylum, someone must be considered a refugee, meaning a person who has suffered persecution, particularly at the hands of his or her country of origin's government. Those seeking asylum must fill out a special form and prove that there is a real fear for their safety if they were to return to their birth country. This form of relief gives someone legal permission to live and work in the country indefinitely, as well as work toward becoming a permanent, legal resident. Those who are seeking or are granted asylum may also petition to bring immediate family members to the country, including children younger than the age of twenty-one.

Withholding of Removal

Withholding of removal is similar to seeking asylum, in that the person requesting this form of relief needs to be a refugee and is trying to avoid persecution. However, instead of requesting to stay in the United States, someone who receives withholding of removal makes a case to not be sent back to his or her country of origin should he or she be ordered to leave the country. These people may be eligible to work in the United States under a visa that has to be renewed annually, but that is all. They do not have the same avenues toward permanent resident status or citizenship that asylum candidates have, and the threat of being deported to a third country always hangs over their heads.

Cancellation of Removal

A cancellation of removal is precisely what its name implies. At the immigration judge's discretion, someone facing deportation can have that action cancelled. Permanent and nonpermanent residents of the United States must meet different qualifications in order to obtain cancellation of removal. Those who have permanent resident status must be able to prove that they have been legal residents for at least five years before receiving a Notice to Appear, have lived in the United States for seven years continuously since becoming a permanent resident, and has not been convicted of a felony. Those holding a temporary visa must have been in the country for ten years, continuously, before receiving their Notice to Appear; be able to prove they have been good people who abide by the law for those ten years; not have been convicted of fraud, moral offenses (such as sex crimes or domestic violence), or an aggravated felony; and have a family member, who is a US citizen or lawful permanent resident, who would suffer extreme hardship if the undocumented immigrant was removed from the country.

Voluntary Removal

Another form of relief comes at the discretion of the defendant in deportation proceedings, rather than that of the judge. By volunteering to leave the country, deportable immigrants or permanent residents have the order of removal against them dropped. Instead, they are given a certain number of days to get their affairs in order and leave. The advantage of voluntary removal for the alien is that it does not place restrictions on them trying to legally enter the country at a later date. Other forms of deportation generally require that the person who has been deported not attempt legal reentry for a set time period, usually between five and twenty years. Voluntary removal can be entered into either before or during deportation proceedings against an individual.

Expedited Removal

There are certain instances in which an immigration proceeding is not necessary to remove aliens who are suspected or guilty of entering the United States illegally. Under an order for expedited removal, the Department of Homeland Security is authorized to remove people from the country immediately if they try to enter through an official port of entry using fake or expired documents. Ports of entry include border checkpoints, international airports, and shipping ports. These are locations where customs or border agents require people to show documents that identify them as US citizens, legal permanent residents, or documented visitors/temporary residents in order to be allowed in the country. Undocumented immigrants may be subject to expedited removal if they are discovered in the country up to two years after their arrival. People who cross a land border illegally may be removed immediately upon being discovered, up to fourteen days after the crossing and within one hundred miles (161 kilometers) of where they entered.

Merits Hearings

Failure to apply for or obtain any form of relief during the master calendar hearing usually leads to a merits hearing being held. By definition, hearings are a chance to share one's side of the story; in other words, to be heard. During a merits hearing is the time for this to happen. Also called simply an individual hearing, the merits hearing is a lot like a criminal trial. Each side presents evidence and calls witnesses to back up their claims. Lawyers for the Department of Homeland Security and ICE seek to prove that the defendant violated immigration laws in such a way as to warrant his or her removal from the country. The defendant will try to convince the judge that either a mistake has been made with regard to identity or immigration status, or that he or she has been a good person and deserves a chance to stay in the country legally.

If the judge finds in favor of the government, then an official Order of Removal is issued. Agents from ICE may take an alien into custody right

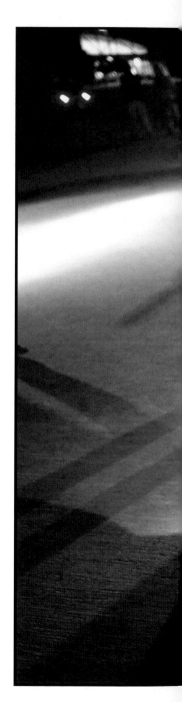

Undocumented immigrants are taken into custody prior to deportation. Shackles prevent people from bolting as they board transportation that will take them to their home country.

from the courthouse as soon as the judge has entered the Order of Removal into the official record. However, this is not always the case. Anyone who has an Order of Removal against him or her has the right to appeal the judge's decision. Once defendants declare their intention to appeal, they are automatically given thirty days to do so.

Failure to file a successful appeal or appeals within that time frame makes the Order of Removal final and gives ICE the green light to remove the person from the country. ICE sends a notice demanding that deportees turn themselves in to be taken into custody prior to deportation. Because the letter explains that the deportee is allowed to bring a small bag of personal belongings with them, the notice is called a Bag and Baggage letter. The agency has ninety days to enforce a final Order of Removal.

Myths & FACTS

About Undocumented Immigrants and Deportation

Myth: People who are found to be in the United States illegally are automatically deported.

Fact: Some undocumented immigrants face expedited removal. Most, however, are subject to the deportation process, which involves a number of steps and, depending on the individual case, may take a while to resolve. Backlogs in the immigration courts may also delay deportation.

Myth: Only undocumented immigrants who sneak over the US border need to worry about deportation.

Fact: Researchers at the Center for Migration Studies found that between 2007 and 2014, more people were in the United States illegally because of expired

(continued on the next page)

(continued from the previous page)

temporary visas than had crossed the border without legal documentation. Those guilty of letting their visas lapse may also be candidates for deportation.

Myth: The majority of undocumented immigrants facing deportation are dangerous, hardened criminals, and that is why they are being removed from the country.

Fact: The Migration Policy Institute reports that approximately 820,000 of the 11 million undocumented immigrants in the United States were found guilty of committing a criminal offense. Less than 3 percent of the total number, however, were convicted of felonies, which are what Homeland Security and ICE officially target as deportable offenses. According to immigration and deportation numbers, many people who have not committed felonies get swept up in the process as well.

Coping with Deportation on Several Fronts

Deportation is a major life event, and as such, it has a huge effect on the lives of everyone it touches. Obviously, the person being removed is affected, but so are his or her family, friends, and even in some cases, employers, coworkers, and neighbors—essentially anyone whose lives would be altered by the deportee's absence. That leaves several to many people left dealing with the upheaval caused by every single case of deportation.

Coping with deportation can seem overwhelming, from the mere threat of being removed to having the threat become a reality, and picking up the pieces after deportation has taken place. Immigration law and sentiment being what they are, particularly in the United States, people can feel powerless against the threat of deportation. But, in truth, they are not. There are ways people can take comfort and find strength even while going through a number of troublesome situations brought about by the threat of deportation.

Issues Faced

The manner in which people are affected by the removal process is multilayered, affecting mind, body, and spirit. Deportation often takes an emotional toll, causing depression and anxiety. The strain and stress of the situation may give rise to physical ills, from mild aches and pains to serious and deadly afflictions such as heart attack and stroke. Less talked about, but arguably quite powerful, are the social and developmental negative effects associated with forcible removal.

As if dealing with such personal issues is not enough, individuals and families facing deportation also must contend with more practical matters that are not working in their favor. These include dealing with a legal system that can easily overwhelm people from a foreign land and culture, a situation that sometimes is complicated further because of a language barrier. Financial matters come into play as well. Many undocumented immigrants, even those who have been

Deportation is an emotional issue, in more ways than one. Deportees and their loved ones often get depressed and anxious when facing removal from the country.

able to find work in their new country, have trouble making ends meet. Add to that the need to hire a lawyer and mount a legal defense against deportation. and money woes get substantially worse. When a wage earner gets deported, a family's budget can either take a nosedive or disappear altogether if, as is often the case, that person was the sole supporter of the household.

Although not foolproof, there are ways to cope with such troublesome developments. What follows are suggested strategies for dealing with the health-related, social, financial, and legal ramifications of threatened and actual deportation.

Stressed Out

Everyone, no matter their lot in life, is bound to run into their fair share of stress. Amounts of stress can increase and decrease, depending on what's happening around them. Usually, people have breaks where their stress decreases in order to give their minds and bodies a chance to recuperate from being under pressure. There are cases where stress levels are pretty high most of the time and for long stretches of time. People living or fighting in a war zone, with the constant threat of attack, injury, or death hanging over their heads, are one example of being under extreme, long-lived stress.

Undocumented immigrants and those living in a country past their visas are another group of people

Stress is never good, but it is especially harmful over long periods. The stress of being in the country illegally takes a definite physical and mental toll on undocumented immigrants.

with dangerous stress levels. The tension caused while trying to remain under the radar, in order to avoid being caught and deported, is tremendous. Events such as witnessing an ICE raid or having someone they know being arrested or detained adds even more stress because it drives home the threat of the same thing happening to them.

Facing the threat of deportation can make a person physically sick. Arrest and removal also can make the body's systems go haywire.

Children especially feel the strain. Even if they were born in the United States and, as citizens, are not themselves in danger of being deported, they live with the fear that a parent or grandparent who is in the country illegally might get caught and be removed. They are in danger of developing what is known as separation anxiety, which is the fear of being separated from a parent or similar adult caretaker.

Living under this cloud of fear often causes anxiety disorders, which are medically recognized mental illnesses that go beyond merely feeling nervous. Most people call them phobias or "panic attacks." The stress from deportation concerns can also easily lead to depression. Both anxiety and depression affect more than the mind; there can be bodily fallout from extreme stress as well. Common complaints associated with these mental conditions include muscle pain, headaches, and gastrointestinal problems. Raised blood pressure and heart rate, which can lead to heart attack and strokes, are also reported.

The Science of Toxic Brains

Since the 1990s, a number of scientific studies have shown that chemicals released during extremely stressful situations can actually change a child's developing brain. The cells of the brain communicate with one another through synapses, creating neural pathways that send messages to different parts of the body. An overload of stress hormones known as methyls can keep neural pathways from developing in parts of the brain that regulate learning and reasoning. Methyls can also make existing synapses weak and ineffective in those areas.

Experts put the stress associated with a parent being deported in the category of extreme stress, causing the release of a lot of these chemicals that can damage learning centers of the brain. The result of this "toxic stress" is behavioral problems in younger children, such as trouble sleeping, throwing tantrums, and soiling themselves. The brains of older kids get so used to the excess amount of hormones that it is almost as if the brain cannot shut off feelings of stress and anxiety.

Complicating matters is the fact that undocumented immigrants and their families may not seek medical help for these conditions. Studies have shown that the mental and physical issues related to stress may go untreated in such individuals because they are afraid that going to the doctor or a hospital will somehow reveal their secret—that they are in the country illegally. Without treatment, their situation often goes from bad to worse.

Coping with Stress

Stress caused by deportation can be bad news. Luckily, there is also good news on that front in the form of ways to cope with the toxic effects of this extreme emotion. Avenues include seeking psychotherapy, leaning on a personal support system, and engaging in self-help.

Getting assistance from a licensed mental health care provider, in the form of therapy and medication, can be very beneficial in defusing emotional tension. Because of privacy laws and medical codes of ethics, health care professionals cannot divulge information about their patients to the authorities. Therefore, even if a doctor or therapist discovers that a patient is undocumented, that information remains confidential by law.

Some people affected by deportation may be eligible for health insurance that covers part of the cost

Undocumented immigrants can rest assured that most health care professionals are more concerned with helping them than they are with a patient's immigration status.

for these services. These include individuals whose employers offer benefits (remember, they may have obtained their job using fake documents) and students whose college or university offers a student health plan. For those who cannot obtain insurance, because of cost or fear of revealing their undocumented status, low-cost options do exist through community and medical/dental school clinics—provided they live near or otherwise have access to these places of course.

For those who cannot afford professional care, or are concerned about sharing information about their immigration status, reaching out to others is a useful substitute for talking to a licensed therapist. Friends and family are usually willing to lend an ear. Because these people know what someone dealing with deportation issues is going through—and possibly because they are in a similar or identical situation themselves—it is a safe bet that a stressed person can trust them with his or her feelings and secrets. Teachers and religious leaders can also be sympathetic listeners, and as a bonus, the nature of their jobs ensures confidentiality.

Another way to help relieve the stress associated with deportation is to, quite literally, take good care of oneself. Some people get active, turning to activities such as exercise, sports, or dancing, as a way to blow off steam and reduce the pressure they feel. Others get very still, engaging in meditation to help clear their minds. Still others find great comfort in their faith and prayer. Basically, whatever positive steps a stressed-out person takes to feel stronger and better about him- or herself is a step in the right direction.

On the Fringes of Society

Compounding the ill effects brought about by toxic stress is the fact that many undocumented immigrants face difficult social issues as well. These are issues that affect how people interact with each other, in their communities and within society in general. In short, deportation, or the threat of deportation, typically causes great upheaval in the way undocumented immigrants and their families live their lives.

Being stopped by the police is an occurrence that undocumented immigrants rightly dread. There is always the chance that their immigration status will be revealed during questioning.

For one thing, those who are in the country illegally are much more likely to "lay low," meaning they tend to keep to themselves and keep out of the public eye as much as possible so that there is less chance of their illegal status coming to light. Something as simple as driving to the store to pick up a few groceries can be fraught with danger for undocumented immigrants. A traffic stop for something as minor as a broken tail light could reveal that the driver does not have a valid license, which leads to a background check and the eventual discovery that the person is in the country illegally.

Being a happy, contributing member of society is hard when someone feels unsafe and is not sure whom to trust. As stated in a 2013 report by the nonprofit public health group Human Impact Partners, "Deportation policy creates a climate of fear and paralysis in communities. People are afraid to drive, afraid to use parks and exercise outdoors, afraid to use public services like clinics, and afraid to get involved in their communities."

Discrimination is another social woe faced by undocumented immigrants. Racism and discrimination exist, to varying degrees and on several levels, throughout virtually every society in the world. Unfortunately, people who are considered "the other" in a society are treated poorly, to say the least. Immigrants are obvious outsiders, who are looked upon with suspicion by some. Add that "the other" may

Social Disconnect

A 2017 study on US-born children of undocumented parents yielded disturbing information about how detention and deportation can affect a person's sense of belonging, even within his or her own family. Even though these children were citizens by virtue of being born in the United States, they reported feeling lost, as if they did not belong either in the United States or the country of their parents' origin. Additionally, society's view of them seemed to be strongly tied to the illegal status of their parents. Many reported feelings of marginalization and exclusion, which caused them to cut themselves off more from society.

Once either or both parents had been deported, the citizen-children, as they are called, felt excluded from the level of social and economic privilege they should have enjoyed as US citizens. Deportation not only separated these children from their parents geographically but also socially. As one study participant noted when comparing herself to her undocumented parents, "I feel that we are kind of different because I'm American, and they are not."

also be committing a crime by being in the country illegally, and anger and discrimination are bound to rear their ugly heads.

One of the most damaging social aspects of deportation is the breakdown of the family unit. Work available to the majority of undocumented immigrants can be highly sporadic, including seasonal labor. So workers need to move around in order to either keep a job or find an opportunity to make more money. Often this involves one parent—typically the father—striking out on his own, separating himself from family members in order to support them. This pales in comparison to the separation brought about by deportation. Seasonal work can be a temporary situation, while deportation means being apart from loved ones for years, if not permanently.

Managing Social Roadblocks

There are ways to change how a society, or at least a portion of society, views undocumented immigrants and the circumstances that brought them to the country illegally. However, this is an uphill battle, and methods are not always effective. In the short term, a better way to cope with social issues connected to deportation may be for undocumented immigrants and their families to alter how they respond to the mistreatment by and misunderstanding of others.

Those who could face deportation often gravitate toward people who are in the same situation. The risk of being found out is lessened, and they can rely on each other for support.

For instance, rather than trying to seamlessly weave oneself into the fabric of everyday life within society at large, undocumented immigrants might be better off either joining or forming a smaller community of people who are in the same situation as they are. These networks of undocumented people can be actual, physical communities, such as neighborhoods, or groups that come together through a connected experience or source, such as work or an immigration rights organization. Either way, such groups form a support system that helps people get through tough situations such as deportation. Communities of undocumented immigrants are an example of the belief that there is "strength in numbers." Each member trusts that others in the community will look out for them and help in any way they can. This support can range from alerting the community when ICE raids are taking place to caring for family members left behind when someone is detained or deported.

Aligning oneself with a community of like-minded and similarly situated people can also be an effective initial defense against discrimination. However, people cannot totally lock themselves away inside a supportive community. Out in the wider world, prejudice and intolerance are probably going to be an issue when deportation is involved. The American Psychological Association recommends that people take a multistep approach to dealing with discrimination that involves focusing on one's strengths and beliefs, building a support system of family and friends, taking part in antidiscrimination organizations and activities, and taking time to calm oneself, so as to think before acting, and planning how one will react to discrimination in the future.

As for how to cope with separation from a family member who has been deported, keeping the lines of communication open is of the utmost importance. This can mean writing letters, making phone calls, and taking advantage of electronic and social media, such as Skype or Facebook. Visits to the deported person in his or her country of origin can keep families close, although friends and family who are themselves in the United States illegally may not want to take this step for fear of not being allowed back in the country. It is recommended that US-born children of undocumented immigrants who have been deported and those who have temporary resident status should seek the advice of an immigration lawyer before traveling outside of the United States to a deported parent's home country.

Money Woes

Economically speaking, deportation is a costly proposition. In 2012, the United States spent $18 billion total on immigration enforcement. In 2017,

Deportation and the Bottom Line

A 2015 report by the group American Action Forum found that the United States federal government would wind up spending approximately $400 billion in order to make mass deportation happen. In the end, such a move would actually cost US taxpayers even more because the gross domestic product (GDP) of the country would take a major hit—to the tune of about $1 trillion. An important economic indicator, GDP is the value of finished goods and services a country produces in a given year, which translates to possible sources of money being pumped into the economy. A majority of undocumented immigrants hold some kind of job, thereby contributing goods and services to the US economy. If those workers are deported, the value of the goods and services they had provided goes with them. The nation's GDP would drop accordingly, putting the country in economic peril.

Congress proposed spending billions more than that, mostly to accommodate the hiring of more ICE and CBP agents and to beef-up security measures, such as a wall along the US-Mexico border. According to CNN,

United States taxpayers paid, on average, $10,845 for each deportation procedure conducted by ICE in 2016. That includes the cost of arresting, detaining, and transporting a person back to his or her country of origin, plus associated immigration court costs.

Those who are being deported and their families, many of whom could already be classified as "the working poor," also pay a steep price. As mentioned, those who are arrested have to post bond if they want to be released from custody while their deportation proceedings are in the works. That amount is usually $1,500 minimum—which is a lot of money for people who are struggling to make ends meet. Added to that is the cost of a lawyer to help present the immigrant's case during court hearings. If the person winds up being deported, his or her family loses that person's salary from any job held in the United States. The situation goes from worse to dire if the deported person was the only one in the family with an income.

Coping with Deportation Expenses

The best way for those facing deportation to cope with financial troubles is to investigate, and then take advantage of, any and all free or inexpensive services available to them. This can begin with receiving help from a pro bono lawyer at the initial appearance in immigration court. In most cases, lawyers who have volunteered their services (usually as part of a longstanding practice of offering several hours of free legal services to individuals in need each year) are available to represent undocumented immigrants facing deportation at their master calendar hearings, free of charge. Any defendant who has not yet hired a lawyer will be appointed one to help him or her navigate the system at the very beginning of the deportation process. However, these pro bono lawyers are only temporary. After the master calendar hearing, those who are in danger of being deported need to hire their own lawyer if they require legal representation.

There are proimmigration organizations that can help potential deportees find lawyers who will take on their cases for little to no money. The only trouble with these sources is that lawyers who charge low fees for handling deportation proceedings are in high demand. Sometimes undocumented immigrants who qualify for this type of legal representation are turned away because the lawyers just cannot handle the workload. Contacting a number of these organizations and the lawyers they recommend is one's best bet for finding affordable legal help. In addition, pro bono lawyers assigned during the master calendar hearing also may be able to recommend legal colleagues who charge reasonable rates.

Regarding how to cope financially after deportation, perhaps the best advice for undocumented immigrants and their families is the same as it would be for legal citizens wanting to avoid having money issues—save. This may be easier said than done for people who are just scraping by on a minimal salary or sending money home to loved ones in their country of origin. But setting aside even a little bit of one's take-home pay every week adds up over time. Think of it as insurance against something bad happening, including being deported.

It used to be that working undocumented immigrants would get paid in cash, which they would place in bags or boxes and hide around their home or keep stashed on their person. Not only did this system open themselves up to theft, but it was not smart financial policy. These days many such workers have discovered the benefits of opening up bank accounts. The money is safer, and having an account helps build a personal financial history that makes things like renting an apartment and paying bills much easier and often less expensive.

Undocumented immigrants would not have a Social Security number, which is required for many financial transactions. However, there are other forms of identification that are accepted by banks and credit unions to establish an account. One of the most popular seems to be an Individual Taxpayer Identification Number (ITIN). Issued by the Internal Revenue Service (IRS), the ITIN was originally created so that foreign

Some undocumented immigrants may work "under the table," meaning they do not report their earnings and are paid in cash. This is one way to help keep their immigration status secret.

nationals doing business in the United States, who were not eligible for Social Security benefits, would have a way to have their tax payments recorded. The IRS does not share the information it receives from applicants, so undocumented immigrants should feel fairly safe in getting an ITIN and using it as a form of ID. An added benefit of the ITIN is that it allows undocumented immigrants to pay taxes, which shows that while they may be in the country illegally, they otherwise are trying to behave in a law-abiding manner while living in the United States.

Avoiding Deportation Through Legal Means

Coping with deportation from a legal standpoint largely involves finding loopholes or otherwise working within the system to avoid deportation. Collectively, these measures are referred to as relief from removal. (Asylum, cancellation of removal, and judicial discretionary relief have been mentioned in a previous section, but the specifics are worth reviewing again as legal coping mechanisms.) Some of these methods apply only in certain circumstances, and most have conditions attached to them. All require strong proof to make the case that a person should be allowed to remain in the country.

Undocumented immigrants who have been arrested and received a notice to appear in immigration court may petition to be granted asylum. Defendants must prove that there is a legitimate fear of persecution in their home countries for asylum to be granted. Proving persecution might also provide grounds for prosecutorial discretion. This is when the person or agency trying to have someone deported decides not to prosecute to the full extent of the law—meaning not pursue deportation even if the person is guilty of breaking immigration laws. Often prosecutorial discretion is granted because of humanitarian reasons such as grave threats to the undocumented immigrant's safety and physical/emotional well-being. Immigration judges are also allowed to grant discretionary relief.

A cancellation of removal may be granted to a green card holder facing deportation after providing proof that he or she legally entered the country at least seven years prior, has had a green card for at least five years, and has never been convicted of an aggravated felony. Once the order of removal has been cancelled, green card holders automatically receive permanent resident status. Rarely do undocumented immigrants receive a cancellation of removal, but those who do must show that they have been in the country at least ten years with a clean criminal record and that their removal would put a heavy burden on a family member who is a US citizen or permanent resident.

Undocumented immigrants who have been the victim of certain crimes may be eligible for a U-visa. This type of visa will be granted only to those who have reported the crime to the police and cooperated during the investigation of the matter and potential prosecution of the perpetrator. Proving that severe emotional or physical trauma has taken place as a result of the crime is also required, as is a clean personal criminal record. Applicants who successfully obtain a U-visa, or a related T-visa (for victims of human trafficking), are then eligible to apply for legal residency through normal channels.

If all else fails, those being deported should consider volunteering to remove themselves from the country. Voluntary removal looks better on a person's record and leaves the door open to documented immigration in the future, without heavy restrictions.

Getting a Lawyer

Experts advise that people in deportation proceedings not attempt to get legal relief on their own. Rather, they should hire an experienced immigration lawyer. Any state bar association should be able to provide the names of and contact information for lawyers who may be able to take on new immigration cases.

Immigration attorneys often offer their services at a reduced cost or even for free. People facing deportation should not be afraid to ask for help finding a lawyer.

Even the federal government, which may seem to be an adversary of undocumented immigrants in deportation proceedings, offers some assistance in finding a lawyer. The United States Department of Justice's Executive Office for Immigration Review (EOIR) offers advice for and leads toward finding competent, affordable legal representation. The EOIR maintains a list of pro bono lawyers, broken down by state, which is updated four times a year.

10 Great Questions
to Ask an
Immigration Lawyer

1. What is the fee for your services?

2. How long have you been practicing immigration law?

3. How many cases like mine have you tried, and what were the outcomes?

4. What exactly am I being charged with?

5. What forms/paperwork do I need to fill out before my next court appearance, and will you help me with that?

6. Am I eligible for any programs, waivers, or exclusions that I can use to keep from being deported?

7. Should I start working on getting my green card while working through the deportation process?

8. How long do you think the deportation process will last?

9. What are my options for appeal if the judge decides I should be deported?

10. What kind of legal preparation can you help me with that will make sure my loved ones are taken care of should I get deported?

More Helpful Tips

Having a decent handle on the emotional, social, financial, and legal aspects of deportation is an important part of dealing with its effects. But there are additional coping mechanisms that those affected by the threat of removal should consider trying as well. Undocumented immigrants should be aware of the rights they have under United States law, plan for the possibility of being detained or deported, and also be on guard against people who want to take advantage of their immigration status. They and their loved ones must be willing to take action against harsh or unfair treatment by immigration officials and the general public, and advocate for themselves and immigration reform. Last but not least, those facing the threat of deportation should not be afraid to seek help from various sources.

Police officers may question someone they believe is in the country illegally. However, undocumented immigrants, like other criminal suspects, have the right not to answer those questions.

The Rights Stuff

Because of their immigration status, people who are in the country illegally are not afforded all of the same rights as US citizens. Yet there are certain situations in which undocumented immigrants legally should be treated like everyone else. In the United States, those accused of crimes have certain rights—as do those being investigated or detained by ICE.

Undocumented immigrants have the right to remain silent. If they are stopped by the police or ICE agents, they do not have to say anything about their immigration status, even if questioned directly. To avoid confusion and make sure there is no misunderstanding, people being stopped should probably let the officer or agent know that they are invoking their right to remain silent. Keeping quiet goes hand-in-hand with their right not to incriminate themselves in any criminal act, including being in the country illegally.

Legally, ICE agents cannot enter a suspected undocumented person's home without good reason, legally referred to as probable cause. In the case of illegal immigration, officers and agents should have information or evidence that would lead someone to reasonably believe a crime had been or was being committed. They also cannot enter without producing a search warrant signed by a judge, which they can get after proving probable cause. The American Civil Liberties Union (ACLU) stresses that a deportation order is not the same thing as a warrant. The order does not allow officers to enter one's home and search for evidence without the resident's consent.

Minus a signed warrant, undocumented immigrants also can refuse to have their car searched if they are stopped while driving. The operator of the vehicle should produce any documents an officer may typically ask for during a traffic stop: a driver's license, registration card, and proof of insurance.

After being stopped in public, undocumented immigrants have the right to ask if they are under arrest. If not, then they should ask to leave the scene of the stop. Once they have been given permission to leave, they should walk calmly and quietly away. Passengers in a stopped car may also follow this example, but the driver should remain until released or arrested.

If an arrest occurs, experts recommend that undocumented immigrants detained by ICE or the police give agents only their name and birth date. They should not engage in any conversations regarding where they were born or how they got in the country without a lawyer present. Neither should the person who is detained or arrested sign anything without first speaking to a legal representative.

Speaking of lawyers, undocumented immigrants also have the right to an attorney. Unlike US citizens, however, people who are in the country illegally must hire their own lawyer. One will not be appointed to represent them.

Fraud Alert

Undocumented immigrants must be on guard to avoid cases of fraud. Unfortunately, con artists want to take advantage of their situation to make money. Common scams include unqualified people offering legal services, requests for payment to process forms and visas, and false claims that someone has won the US State Department's green card Diversity Lottery.

Undocumented immigrants seeking relief from deportation should trust only legitimate sources of assistance whose credentials can be checked. With regard to legal services, that primarily means a licensed attorney or an approved member of the Board of Immigration Appeals, a federal organization that decides matters concerning appealed immigration cases. Representatives of the person's home country consulate also qualify. Those who don't include law students (unless supervised by a licensed attorney and working pro bono), notary publics, and so-called immigration consultants.

Undocumented immigrants should never send money to an individual claiming to represent the federal government regarding the issuance of a green card. The USCIS and other legitimate federal offices do not accept PayPal, payment by phone or telegram, or checks written to individuals by name.

Hope for the Best, Prepare for the Worst

People plan for all sorts of things that will or could possibly happen. Examples include saving money for college or retirement, conducting fire drills, writing a will, and so on. By planning, they hope not to get caught in a bad situation because they were unprepared. Even if things do get negative, planning can help cushion the blow and make things better. Anyone who is in the country illegally understands that he or she could get caught breaking immigration law and be deported. With that in mind, many undocumented immigrants choose to make plans regarding what should happen to them and their loved ones if they are removed from the United States.

At the top of the preparation list for those who could face deportation is providing for their children. There is real worry within the undocumented community that US-born minors (those younger than eighteen years of age) can wind up in the foster care system if both parents are unable to care for them due to detainment or deportation. In order to help keep their children in the United States and out of foster care, some undocumented immigrants sign paperwork naming a friend or relative as legal guardian of their kids. Ideally, the guardian should be a legal citizen of

So that they are prepared in case they are deported, undocumented immigrants would be wise to consider signing a power of attorney.

the United States or at least someone who has a green card and is a permanent resident.

Similar legal papers can give another person power of attorney over any property an undocumented immigrant might own. This includes land, homes, businesses, or vehicles. A power of attorney gives someone the right to make legal decisions regarding such items if the original owner is not able to do so. Handling matters such as selling a house or car and running a business is difficult, if not impossible, to do when a person is detained or removed from the country. Having the peace of mind that comes with knowing one's possessions are in good hands should immigration troubles arise is a good way to help people cope with a deportation threat.

Demonstrated Beliefs

For centuries, people have gathered together in public to let their voices be heard in protest. Staging or taking part in a protest march is an effective and, hopefully, peaceful form of self-expression. Standing up for what one believes is right, particularly while standing with people who have the same beliefs, is a reliable coping mechanism.

Protests in favor of the country adopting laws that take into account the human dignity of undocumented immigrants are nothing new. Yet as the debate over immigrants in the United States has heated up,

Activists protest in favor of reinstating the DREAM Act in Washington in 2017. Letting their voices be heard helps immigrants better cope with the threat of deportation.

especially in the first two decades of the twenty-first century, the frequency and size of protests has grown accordingly. In 2006, massive rallies occurred in cities across the United States protesting a proposed change to US immigration policy. In 2014, protesters filled US city streets again, including those of Washington, DC, marching both for and against immigration reform. Then there were protests against US president Donald Trump's stepped-up immigration enforcement policies and the rescinding of DACA in 2017. On

May 1 of that year, Latino immigrants staged "A Day Without Immigrants," a multicity work strike and pro-immigrant rights march.

Protesting can do more than let someone voice his or her opinion. People pay attention when protests take place, especially if a large number of marchers participate or the topic is extremely controversial. The news media cover these events, and more people consider joining or supporting whatever cause is being protested. More important, well-organized, thoughtful protests can get the attention of those who have the power to make real change. In the case of immigration reform, that could be members of the federal government, who can issue executive orders, rewrite laws in Congress, or interpret existing laws with a renewed sense of discretion. Even if the result is not immediate immigrant reform, protests at the very least open up discussions about the topic at hand.

Resistance May Not Be Futile

Beyond talking about or calling attention to immigration issues through protesting is a step called resistance, which is where people disobey or ignore laws and unwritten rules that they believe are unjust to take action. Peaceful resistance, which is the type practiced by those who are pro-immigration reform, also has been called civil disobedience.

Sources of Support

As the saying goes, there is strength in numbers. That is why so many causes have support groups, with numerous members, attached to them. Dealing with the threat of deportation is certainly no exception. Many groups and organizations have formed across the country to assist those experiencing the threat of removal from the United States. Some are officially registered nonprofits and immigrant- or human-rights groups, while others are simply grassroots, community-based efforts. Religious and political boundaries are crossed or ignored as churches and other faith groups, bipartisan lawmakers, and local and state governments offer to help undocumented and otherwise deportation-worthy immigrants in their quest to stay in the country.

Their support might be general, covering many areas, or more specific and tailored to a certain element of the deportation process, such as legal aid or physical and mental health counseling. They may organize volunteers who rush to locations where immigration raids are occurring, serving as witnesses that no one's rights are infringed in the

(continued on the next page)

(continued from the previous page)

process. They may set up a kind of "phone tree," warning undocumented immigrants when a raid occurs near them; apps are in development to serve the same purpose via text and social media. Or, as the Mexican consulate did in late 2016, staff a round-the-clock hotline that allows people to report immigration abuses in the United States.

Representatives from the group Network Nuns on the Bus speak to a crowd at the conclusion of a cross-country proimmigration tour.

Examples of individuals and groups of people engaged in resistance include hunger strikes by federal detention center inmates in Texas and Washington state in 2014, high school and college students staging walk-outs and sit-ins on campuses across the nation in 2016, and protesters blocking the entrance to a Philadelphia highway and forming a human chain to stop traffic on New York City's Fifth Avenue in 2017. Some undocumented immigrants have felt so strongly about the need for immigration reform that they have taken part in civil disobedience measures.

Entire communities have joined the resistance movement as cities across the United States have declared themselves sanctuary sites. Sanctuary cities are designed to be safe places for undocumented immigrants because of limited cooperation between local (meaning anything below the federal level) police and ICE. By law, local police must share information on people arrested for reasons not related to their immigration status with federal authorities. Using that information, particularly fingerprints, ICE may uncover someone who is in the country illegally, at which point they would ask that local police hold the person until federal immigration authorities can make an arrest. Police working in sanctuary cities are compelled by written policy or law not to comply with ICE's "detainer requests," citing, among other reasons, their lack of jurisdiction over immigration matters that are legally handled at the federal level.

Some people think acts of resistance are futile, saying that little has changed as a result of people resisting. Even at their weakest, though, resistance has the same effect as protesting, which is to call attention to a matter and start conversations that may eventually bring about real change.

Be an Advocate

Advocates are people who actively work in support of a cause. Protesters are advocates in that they speak out

Advocates share their beliefs in an effort to convince others to join them in a cause. Immigration reform advocates work to change laws they believe are unfair to undocumented people.

publicly in favor of the things they believe are right and just. But there are other avenues to explore for those who are pro-immigrant rights—avenues that can help deal with deportation and detainment threats.

It may sound overly simple, but volunteering can be an excellent outlet for those hoping to counteract the effects of deportation. Manpower is needed in order for immigration reform to move forward and immigrant rights groups to succeed. The more people working on behalf of these causes, the more progress can be made toward achieving the group's goals.

US-born children of undocumented immigrants aged eighteen and older, naturalized US citizens, and citizens who simply believe in the causes of immigration rights and reform can make their feelings known by voting. Going to the polls lets people elect representatives who have the power to pass laws and create policy that affect how immigration laws are enforced and rates of deportation. Additionally, legislation dealing with immigration reform may be featured on the ballot, especially in border states (California, Arizona, etc.) and metropolitan areas where large populations of undocumented immigrants work and live.

Advocating for immigration reform serves a couple of purposes. First, it helps those who are currently under threat of deportation by giving them a positive outlet for their energies and concerns. Second,

Voting lets people put their convictions into action by giving them a voice in government. It is a good way to change laws that affect those who may face deportation.

it attempts to help future generations of immigrants, undocumented or not, by putting a personal face on an issue that affects millions of people.

Many people find that a combination of several different coping methods is the most useful and effective when immigration issues arise. What those methods might be and how large a role each will play depends on a person's circumstances and available resources. In the end, each individual facing personal removal or that of a loved one needs to learn how to cope with the threat of deportation in his or her own way.

Glossary

advocate To support or argue for a cause or belief.

affliction An illness or injury that causes hardship or suffering.

alien Belonging or being loyal to another country or government.

asylum A state of protection and safety.

correlate When two items are shown to be similar enough to have an effect on each other.

denaturalized Not having the rights normally given to citizens of a country.

detainment The state of being held in custody.

dictated Issued as an order.

discretionary At someone's personal choice or decision.

felony A serious crime, often involving violence.

futile Not being useful or having a specific purpose.

incriminate To show evidence of a crime having been committed.

intolerance The state of being unable to treat people fairly.

jurisdiction Refers to the authority to apply or enforce laws.

persecution The act of annoying or injuring another person or people.

ramifications The results stemming from an action or decision.

sanctuary A place where people can feel safe.

sporadic Occurring every now and then, on occasion.

synapse The gap over which information is passed from one neuron to another.

violation The act of breaking or ignoring a law or laws.

visa An official document or passport mark that shows the reason someone is in a country other than his or her own.

For More Information

American Civil Liberties Union (ACLU)
125 Broad Street, 18th Floor
New York, NY 10004
(212) 549-2500
Facebook: @aclu
Twitter: @ACLU
Website: https://www.aclu.org

The American Civil Liberties Union has a long history of defending the rights of individuals as defined by the United States Constitution and US law. Among the issues tackled by the ACLU are immigrants' rights, including detention and deportation.

Canadian Council for Refugees
6839 Drolet #302
Montréal, QC H2S 2T1
Canada
(514) 277-7223
Facebook and Twitter: @ccrweb
Website: http://ccrweb.ca/en/home

A national nonprofit, the Canadian Council for Refugees is committed to ensuring the rights of refugees and migrants throughout the provinces. The organization conducts policy analysis and government-relations research, provides networking and professional development opportunities, and engages in public education on topics such as migrant rights.

Center for Immigration Studies
1629 K Street NW, Suite 600
Washington, DC 20006
(202) 466-8185
Facebook: @CenterforImmigrationStudies
Twitter: @wwwCISorg
Website: https://cis.org
The research organization Center for Immigration Studies was founded in 1985. The organization's main goal is to provide reliable information about how legal and illegal immigration affects various aspects of life in the United States.

Fair Immigration Reform Movement
Center for Community Change
1536 U Street NW
Washington, DC 20009
(202) 339-9300
Facebook: @fair.immigration.reform.movement
Twitter: @Re4mimmigration
Website: https://fairimmigration.org
The Fair Immigration Reform Movement is

an umbrella organization for grassroots organizations focused on immigrant rights. The movement leads projects aimed at keeping families together.

Families for Freedom
35 W. 31st Street, No. 702
New York, NY 10010
(646) 290-8720
Facebook: @families4freedom
Twitter: @familiesfreedom
Website: http://familiesforfreedom.org
Based in New York City, Families for Freedom is a human rights organization by and for families facing and fighting deportation. The organization offers support services and education, and runs advocacy campaigns for directly affected families and communities.

Immigration, Refugees and Citizenship Canada
Government of Canada
200 Catherine Street, Suite 101
Ottawa, ON K2P 2K9
Canada
Website: http://www.cic.gc.ca/english/index.asp
Immigration, Refugees and Citizenship Canada

is a government agency that helps immigrants get settled in the country and helps protect the rights of refugees. The agency provides visa and citizenship services, and provides information on living, working, and studying in Canada as an immigrant.

National Immigrant Justice Center
208 S. LaSalle Street, Suite 1300
Chicago, IL 60604
(312) 660-1370
Twitter: @CitImmCanada
Website: https://www.immigrantjustice.org
NIJC provides direct legal services to immigrants, refugees, and asylum seekers. Advocacy services offered include policy reform, litigation, and public education.

National Immigration Forum
50 F Street NW, Suite 300
Washington, DC 20001
(202) 347-0040
Facebook: @NationalImmigrationForum
Twitter: @NatImmForum
Website: http://immigrationforum.org
The National Immigration Forum gathers like-

minded advocates from across the United States to discuss ways to recognize the value of immigrants to the country. The forum supports commonsense immigration reform and balanced, fair enforcement of current immigration laws.

Boehm, Deborah. *Returned: Going and Coming in an Age of Deportation*. Oakland, CA: University of California Press, 2016.

Cunningham, Anne. *Current Controversies: Deporting Immigrants*. New York, NY: Greenhaven Press, 2018.

Denton, Michelle. *Hot Topics: Immigration Issues in America*. New York, NY: Lucent Books/Greenhaven, 2017.

Gay, Kathlyn. *Activism: The Ultimate Teen Guide*. Lanham, MD: Rowman & Littlefield Publishers, 2016.

Haugen, David M. *Human Rights in Focus: Illegal Immigrants*. San Diego, CA: ReferencePoint Press, 2017.

Lusted, Marcia Amidon. *Know Your Rights: Your Legal Rights as an Immigrant*. New York, NY: Rosen Publishing, 2016.

Nazario, Sonia. *Enrique's Journey*. New York, NY: Ember (Random House Children's Books), 2014.

Regan, Margaret. *Detained and Deported: Stories of Immigrant Families Under Fire*. Boston, MA: Beacon Press, 2015.

Saedi, Sara. *Americanized: Rebel Without a Green Card*. New York, NY: Knopf Doubleday, 2018.

Staley, Erin. *Teen Life 411: I'm an Undocumented Immigrant. Now What?* New York, NY: Rosen Publishing, 2017.

Bibliography

American Immigration Council. "The Facts About the Individual Tax Identification Number (ITIN)." April 2016. https://www.americanimmigrationcouncil.org/research/facts-about-individual-tax-identification-number-itin.

Associated Press. "Obama Administration Spent $18B on Immigration Enforcement." *USA Today*, January 2013. https://www.usatoday.com/story/news/nation/2013/01/07/obama-immigration-enforcement/1815667.

Associated Press. "Obama Ends Secure Communities Program That Helped Hike Deportations." NBCNews online, November 2014. https://www.nbcnews.com/storyline/immigration-reform/obama-ends-secure-communities-program-helped-hike-deportations-n253541.

Blanco, Octavio. "How Much Money It Costs ICE to Deport an Undocumented Immigrant." CNN Money, April 2017. http://money.cnn.com/2017/04/13/news/economy/deportation-costs-undocumented-immigrant/index.html.

Bray, Ilona. "Overview of U.S. Deportation/Removal Proceedings." AllLaw.com. Retrieved September 2017. http://www.alllaw.com/articles/nolo/us-immigration/deportation-removal-proceedings.html.

Brondolo, Elizabeth, et al. "Discrimination: What Is It and How to Cope." American Psychological Association. Retrieved October 2017. http://www.apa.org/helpcenter/discrimination.aspx.

Castaneda, Ruben. "Where Can Undocumented Immigrants Go for Health Care?" *U.S. News and World Report*, November 2016. https://health.usnews.com/wellness/articles/2016-11-02/where-can-undocumented-immigrants-go-for-health-care.

Cortes, Luis. *A Simple Guide to U.S. Immigration and Citizenship*. New York, NY: Atria Books, 2008.

Engler, Mark, and Paul Engler. "The Massive Immigrant-Rights Protests of 2006 Are Still Changing Politics." *Los Angeles Times*. March 4, 2016. http://www.latimes.com/opinion/op-ed/la-oe-0306-engler-immigration-protests-2006-20160306-story.html.

Gitis, Ben, and Laura Collins. "The Budgetary and Economic Costs of Addressing Unauthorized Immigration: Alternative Strategies." American Action Forum, March 2015. https://www.americanactionforum.org/research/the-budgetary-and-economic-costs-of-addressing-unauthorized-immigration-alt.

Haugen, David, and Susan Musser, eds. *Opposing Viewpoints: Illegal Immigration*. Farmington Hills, MI: Greenhaven Press, 2011.

Hellerstein, Erica. "How Deportation Affects the Health of Families." Chronicle of Social Change, July 2013. https://chronicleofsocialchange.org /featured/how-deportation-affects-families -mental-and-physical-health.

Khazan, Olga. "The Toxic Health Effects of Deportation Threat." *Atlantic*, January 2017. https://www.theatlantic.com/health /archive/2017/01/the-toxic-health-effects-of -deportation-threat/514718.

Linthicum, Kate. "Mexico Instructs Its Embassy and Consulates in the U.S. to Increase Measures to Protect Immigrants." *Los Angeles Times*, November 16, 2016. http://www.latimes .com/world/mexico-americas/la-fg-mexico -immigrants-20161116-story.html.

McCarthy, Joe, and Phineas Rueckert. "7 Ways You Can Help Undocumented Immigrants Right Now." Global Citizen, September 2017. https:// www.globalcitizen.org/en/content/7-ways-to -help-undocumented-immigrants.

Mennard, William C. "House Spending Bill for Homeland Security Heavy on Border Wall, Enforcement, and Deportation." Norris, McLaughlin, & Marcus blog. July 2017. https:// www.nmmlaw.com/ib/2017/07/13/house -spending-bill-homeland-security-heavy -border-wall-enforcement-deportation.

Scudder, Laurie. "The Black Cloud of Deportation and Stress in Immigrant Children." Medscape, February 2017. https://www.medscape.com/viewarticle/875348_2.

Sheehy, Kelsey. "How Undocumented Immigrants Can Get Bank Accounts." Nerdwallet.com, September 2015. https://www.nerdwallet.com/blog/banking/undocumented-immigrants-bank-accounts.

USA.gov. "Deportation." Retrieved September 2017. https://www.usa.gov/deportation.

USCIS.gov. "Public Charge Fact Sheet." April 2011. https://www.uscis.gov/news/fact-sheets/public-charge-fact-sheet.

US Immigration and Customs Enforcement. "What We Do." Retrieved September 2017. https://www.ice.gov/overview.

Yee, Vivian, et al. "Here's the Reality About Illegal Immigrants in the United States." *New York Times*, March 6, 2017. https://www.nytimes.com/interactive/2017/03/06/us/politics/undocumented-illegal-immigrants.html.

Zayas, Luis H., and Laurie Cook Heffron. "Disrupting Young Lives: How Detention and Deportation Affect U.S.-Born Children of Immigrants." American Psychological Association CYF News, November 2016. http://www.apa.org/pi/families/resources

/newsletter/2016/11/detention-deportation
.aspx.

Zayas, Luis H., and Lauren E. Gulbas. "Process of Belonging for Citizen-Children of Undocumented Mexican Immigrants." *Journal of Child and Family Studies*, September 2017, Volume 26, Issue 9, pp. 2463–2474.

About the Author

A writer and editor living in upstate New York, Jeanne Nagle has spent years researching and writing on topics that, like deportation, affect young adults and their families. Among her works are titles covering drug use and abuse, suicide, and LGBTQ rights.

Photo Credits